Numbers 0 through 10

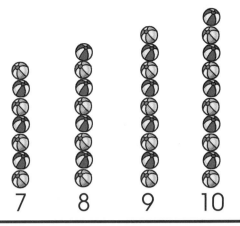

0   1   2   3   4   5   6   7   8   9   10

Circle the number that tells how many.

2   3

5   6

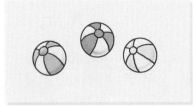

1   2

3   4

5   6

0   1

6   7

8   9

Matching Numbers with Objects

Match the group with the correct numbers.

| 1 |
| 2 |
| 3 |
| 4 |
| 5 |
| 6 |
| 7 |
| 8 |
| 9 |
| 10 |

Drawing Objects for Numbers

Draw the correct number of objects.

2 🍎

7 🍉

6 🍌

5 🥕

3 🍐

9 🍓

10 🍅

8 🍊

Writing Numbers

Trace.

0 1 2 3 4
5 6 7 8 9 10

Write the missing numbers.

0 1 ___ 3
5 ___ 7 ___ 10

Write the numbers **0–10** in order.

Writing Numbers for Objects

Write how many animals are in each group.

 _____

 _____

 _____

 _____

 _____

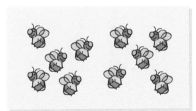 _____

 _____

 _____

Which Group Has More?

 ← This group has **more** penguins.

Circle the group that has **more** animals.

1.

2.

3.

4.

5.

6.

7. Draw a group of 🐟 to show **1 more** than **3**.

How many 🐟? _____

Which Number is Greater?

In math, **greater** means **more than**.
5 is **greater** than 3.

⑤   3

Write how many are in each group. Circle the **greater** number.

1.

_____   _____

2.

_____   _____

3.

_____   _____

4.

_____   _____

5.

_____   _____

6.

_____   _____

Comparing numbers; concept of greater

Which Group Has Fewer?

← This group has **fewer** bats.

Circle the group that has **fewer** animals.

1.

2.

3.

4.

5.
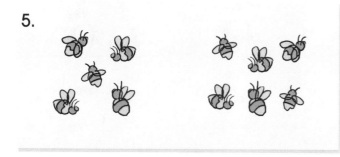

6.

7. Draw a group of 🦋s to show **1 fewer** than 10.

How many 🦋s? _____

Concept of fewer

Which Number is Less?

In math, **less** means **fewer** or **not as many**.
9 is **less** than 10.

⑨   10

Write how many are in each group. Circle the number that is **less**.

1.

   _____   _____

2.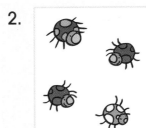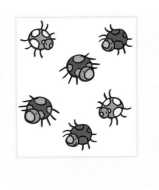

   _____   _____

3.

   _____   _____

4.

   _____   _____

5.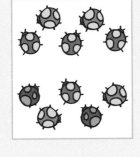

   _____   _____

6.

   _____   _____

Comparing numbers; concept of less

Adding to Find the Sum

$$\underline{}\ 1\ + \underline{}\ 2\ = \underline{}\ 3\ $$ The **sum** tells how many in all.

Write a number sentence about each picture. Find the **sum**.

1.

_____ + _____ = _____

2.

_____ + _____ = _____

3.

_____ + _____ = _____

4.

_____ + _____ = _____

5.

_____ + _____ = _____

6.

_____ + _____ = _____

7.

_____ + _____ = _____

8.

_____ + _____ = _____

More Adding

$$\begin{array}{r} 1 \\ +\ 2 \\ \hline =\ 3 \end{array} \leftarrow \textbf{sum}$$

Complete the problem for each picture. Find the **sum**.

1.

_____
+ _____
= _____

2.

_____
+ _____
= _____

3.

_____
+ _____
= _____

4.

_____
+ _____
= _____

5.

_____
+ _____
= _____

6.

_____
+ _____
= _____

7.

_____
+ _____
= _____

8.

_____
+ _____
= _____

Subtracting to Find the Difference

$$\underline{}\ 5\ \underline{} - \underline{}\ 2\ \underline{} = \underline{\ 3\ }$$

The **difference** tells how many are left.

Write a number sentence about each picture.

1.

_____ - _____ = _____

2.

_____ - _____ = _____

3.

_____ - _____ = _____

4.

_____ - _____ = _____

5.

_____ - _____ = _____

6.

_____ - _____ = _____

7.

_____ - _____ = _____

8.

_____ - _____ = _____

More Subtracting

$$\begin{array}{r} 3 \\ - \ 1 \\ \hline = \ 2 \end{array}$$ ← **difference**

Complete the problem for each picture. Find the **difference**.

1.

$$\begin{array}{r} \underline{} \\ - \ \underline{} \\ = \ \underline{} \end{array}$$

2.

$$\begin{array}{r} \underline{} \\ - \ \underline{} \\ = \ \underline{} \end{array}$$

3.

$$\begin{array}{r} \underline{} \\ - \ \underline{} \\ = \ \underline{} \end{array}$$

4.

$$\begin{array}{r} \underline{} \\ - \ \underline{} \\ = \ \underline{} \end{array}$$

5.

$$\begin{array}{r} \underline{} \\ - \ \underline{} \\ = \ \underline{} \end{array}$$

6.

$$\begin{array}{r} \underline{} \\ - \ \underline{} \\ = \ \underline{} \end{array}$$

7.

$$\begin{array}{r} \underline{} \\ - \ \underline{} \\ = \ \underline{} \end{array}$$

8.

$$\begin{array}{r} \underline{} \\ - \ \underline{} \\ = \ \underline{} \end{array}$$

Addition Facts Table–Sums through 5

Fill in the addition table by finding the **sums**.
Color your answers. Do you see a pattern?

+	0	1	2	3	4	5
0	0					
1						
2				5		
3		4				
4						
5						

2 + 3 = 5

0 = Red

1 = Purple

2 = Blue

3 = Orange

4 = Yellow

5 = Green

Adding and Subtracting

Watch the signs!

Add
$$\begin{array}{r} 3 \\ +1 \\ \hline 4 \end{array}$$

Subtract
$$\begin{array}{r} 3 \\ -1 \\ \hline 2 \end{array}$$

Find the **sum** or **difference**. The addition facts table on page 14 may help you.

1. $3 + 1 =$ _____

2. $3 - 1 =$ _____

3. $2 + 0 =$ _____

4. $5 - 1 =$ _____

5. $2 + 3 =$ _____

6. $4 - 3 =$ _____

7. $2 - 0 =$ _____

8. $1 + 2 =$ _____

9. $4 + 1 =$ _____

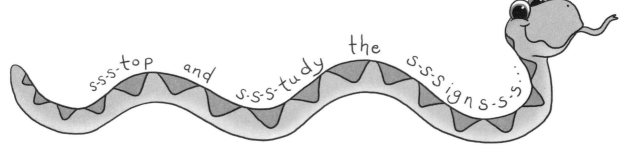

10. $\begin{array}{r} 3 \\ +1 \\ \hline \end{array}$

11. $\begin{array}{r} 2 \\ -1 \\ \hline \end{array}$

12. $\begin{array}{r} 5 \\ +0 \\ \hline \end{array}$

13. $\begin{array}{r} 4 \\ -1 \\ \hline \end{array}$

14. $\begin{array}{r} 3 \\ -2 \\ \hline \end{array}$

15. $\begin{array}{r} 0 \\ +3 \\ \hline \end{array}$

16. $\begin{array}{r} 2 \\ +2 \\ \hline \end{array}$

17. $\begin{array}{r} 3 \\ -0 \\ \hline \end{array}$

Finding Sums 6 through 10

____6____ + ____3____ = ____9____

Write a number sentence about each picture. Find the **sum**.

1.
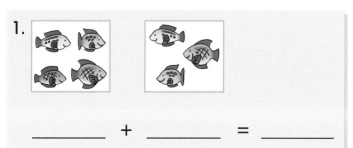

_____ + _____ = _____

2.
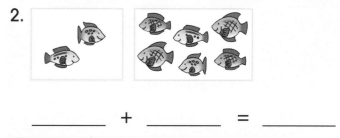

_____ + _____ = _____

3.
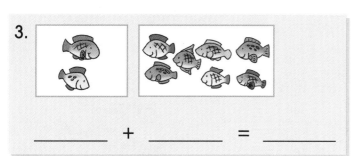

_____ + _____ = _____

4.

_____ + _____ = _____

5.
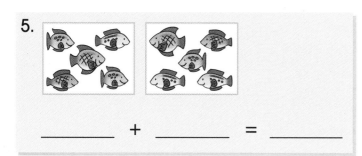

_____ + _____ = _____

6.
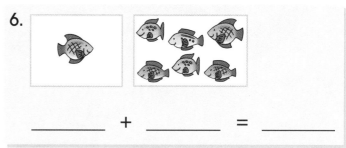

_____ + _____ = _____

7.
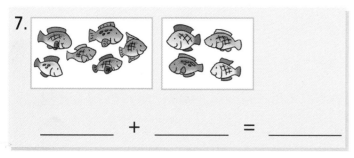

_____ + _____ = _____

8.
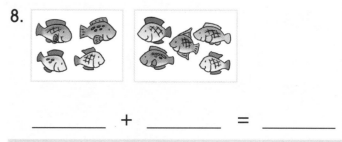

_____ + _____ = _____

Adding On to Find Sums

Add **1** to each number.
Write the answer.

$8 + 1 = 9$

0 1 2 3 4 5 6 7 8 9 10

1. Add **1** to each number.
Write the answer.

6 ____

8 ____

7 ____

9 ____

2. Add **2** to each number.
Write the answer.

5 ____

7 ____

8 ____

6 ____

3. Add **3** to each number.
Write the answer.

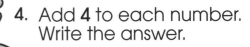

5 ____

6 ____

4 ____

7 ____

4. Add **4** to each number.
Write the answer.

5 ____

3 ____

4 ____

6 ____

Addition Facts Table-Sums through 10

Fill in the addition facts table by finding the **sums**.

+	0	1	2	3	4	5	6	7	8	9
0	0						6			
1										
2						7				
3							10			
4										
5										
6										
7		8								
8										
9										

Write the sums.

$9 + 1 =$ _____

$8 + 2 =$ _____

$7 + 3 =$ _____

$6 + 4 =$ _____

$5 + 5 =$ _____

Addition facts table: sums through10

Addition Fact Pairs

When you know one fact, you can think of another fact.

Look at the addition facts table on page 18.
Find these facts in the table. What do you notice?

$3 + 5 = 8$ $7 + 0 = 7$

$5 + 3 = 8$ $0 + 7 = 7$

Write the **sums**. Use the addition facts table on page 18 if you need to.

1. $6 + 3 =$ _____

3 + 6 = _____

2. $5 + 2 =$ _____

$2 + 5 =$ _____

3. $7 + 3 =$ _____

$3 + 7 =$ _____

4. $9 + 1 =$ _____

$1 + 9 =$ _____

5. $6 + 2 =$ _____

$2 + 6 =$ _____

6. $8 + 0 =$ _____

$0 + 8 =$ _____

Write the **sum**. Then write another addition fact using the same numbers.

7. $4 + 5 =$ _____

_____ + _____ = _____

8. $3 + 4 =$ _____

_____ + _____ = _____

9. $6 + 0 =$ _____

_____ + _____ = _____

10. $8 + 2 =$ _____

_____ + _____ = _____

11. $0 + 9 =$ _____

_____ + _____ = _____

12. $1 + 7 =$ _____

_____ + _____ = _____

Write a pair of addition facts for each group of numbers.

13.   2 7 9

_____ + _____ = _____

_____ + _____ = _____

14.   4 6 10

_____ + _____ = _____

_____ + _____ = _____

15.   0 8 8

_____ + _____ = _____

_____ + _____ = _____

More Subtraction Facts

A number line can help you find **differences**.

$9 - 3 = \underline{6}$

$$\begin{array}{r} 9 \\ -\ 3 \\ \hline 6 \end{array}$$

Count back from **9**.

Find the **differences**. Use the number line if you need to.

1. $8 - 3 = \underline{\hphantom{00}}$ 2. $7 - 2 = \underline{\hphantom{00}}$ 3. $10 - 4 = \underline{\hphantom{00}}$

4. $9 - 1 = \underline{\hphantom{00}}$ 5. $6 - 0 = \underline{\hphantom{00}}$ 6. $8 - 4 = \underline{\hphantom{00}}$

7. $\begin{array}{r} 6 \\ -\ 4 \\ \hline \end{array}$ 8. $\begin{array}{r} 8 \\ -\ 2 \\ \hline \end{array}$ 9. $\begin{array}{r} 5 \\ -\ 5 \\ \hline \end{array}$ 10. $\begin{array}{r} 9 \\ -\ 4 \\ \hline \end{array}$

11. $\begin{array}{r} 10 \\ -\ 3 \\ \hline \end{array}$ 12. $\begin{array}{r} 7 \\ -\ 4 \\ \hline \end{array}$ 13. $\begin{array}{r} 9 \\ -\ 7 \\ \hline \end{array}$ 14. $\begin{array}{r} 10 \\ -\ 8 \\ \hline \end{array}$

15. Write a subtraction equation for this number line.

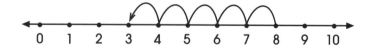

$\underline{\hphantom{000}} - \underline{\hphantom{000}} = \underline{\hphantom{000}}$

Subtraction Fact Pairs

Look at these subtraction facts.

$8 - 3 = 5$ $9 - 0 = 9$

$8 - 5 = 3$ $9 - 9 = 0$

When you know one fact, you can think of another fact.

Write the **differences**.

1. $7 - 3 = $ _____

   $7 - 4 = $ _____

2. $9 - 5 = $ _____

   $9 - 4 = $ _____

3. $7 - 0 = $ _____

   $7 - 7 = $ _____

4. $9 - 1 = $ _____

   $9 - 8 = $ _____

5. $10 - 2 = $ _____

   $10 - 8 = $ _____

6. $8 - 6 = $ _____

   $8 - 2 = $ _____

Write the **difference**. Then write another subtraction fact using the same numbers.

7. $9 - 5 = $ _____

   $9 - 4 = $ ___

8. $7 - 5 = $ _____

   ___ - ___ = ___

9. $6 - 0 = $ _____

   ___ - ___ = ___

10. $10 - 2 = $ _____

    ___ - ___ = ___

11. $8 - 8 = $ _____

    ___ - ___ = ___

12. $8 - 1 = $ _____

    ___ - ___ = ___

Write a pair of subtraction facts for each group of numbers.

13. 3 6 9

    ___ - ___ = ___

    ___ - ___ = ___

14. 2 8 10

    ___ - ___ = ___

    ___ - ___ = ___

15. 0 9 9

    ___ - ___ = ___

    ___ - ___ = ___

Subtraction Fun

Write the **differences**.
Color the picture.

$$\begin{array}{r} 6 \\ -\ 2 \\ \hline \end{array}$$
$$\begin{array}{r} 7 \\ -\ 4 \\ \hline \end{array}$$
$$\begin{array}{r} 8 \\ -\ 4 \\ \hline \end{array}$$
$$\begin{array}{r} 6 \\ -\ 6 \\ \hline \end{array}$$
$$\begin{array}{r} 10 \\ -\ 8 \\ \hline \end{array}$$
$$\begin{array}{r} 8 \\ -\ 8 \\ \hline \end{array}$$
$$\begin{array}{r} 4 \\ -\ 4 \\ \hline \end{array}$$
$$\begin{array}{r} 9 \\ -\ 5 \\ \hline \end{array}$$
$$\begin{array}{r} 7 \\ -\ 2 \\ \hline \end{array}$$
$$\begin{array}{r} 9 \\ -\ 4 \\ \hline \end{array}$$
$$\begin{array}{r} 6 \\ -\ 1 \\ \hline \end{array}$$
$$\begin{array}{r} 10 \\ -\ 6 \\ \hline \end{array}$$
$$\begin{array}{r} 9 \\ -\ 6 \\ \hline \end{array}$$
$$\begin{array}{r} 8 \\ -\ 6 \\ \hline \end{array}$$
$$\begin{array}{r} 7 \\ -\ 3 \\ \hline \end{array}$$
$$\begin{array}{r} 10 \\ -\ 9 \\ \hline \end{array}$$
$$\begin{array}{r} 8 \\ -\ 5 \\ \hline \end{array}$$
$$\begin{array}{r} 10 \\ -\ 5 \\ \hline \end{array}$$

0 = Red
1 = Purple
2 = Blue
3 = Orange
4 = Yellow
5 = Green

22   Differences related to sums through 10

Adding and Subtracting

Add **+**

Subtract **−**

Watch out for the signs!

Find the **sum** or **difference**.

1. 8 + 1 = _____

2. 7 − 2 = _____

3. 9 + 0 = _____

4. 10 − 1 = _____

5. 6 + 3 = _____

6. 8 − 3 = _____

7. 8 − 0 = _____

8. 7 + 2 = _____

9. 4 + 6 = _____

Be-e-e-e sure to watch those signs

10.
```
   1
 + 9
```

11.
```
   5
 − 1
```

12.
```
   7
 + 0
```

13.
```
   9
 − 2
```

14.
```
   3
 − 0
```

15.
```
   3
 + 7
```

16.
```
   5
 + 5
```

17.
```
   6
 − 0
```

Numbers 11 through 20

11   12   13   14   15   16   17   18   19   20

Match.

Circle groups of 10.

	10 and More	**Number**
1.	10 and 3	11
		12
2.	10 and 5	13
		14
3.	10 and 1	15
		16
4.	10 and 7	17
		18
5.	10 and 10	19
6.	10 and 6	20

Counting to 20

1 through 10	1	2	3	4	5	6	7	8	9	10
11 and more	11	12	13	14	15	16	17	18	19	20

Write the missing numbers.

1. 11, 12 _____ , 14, _____ , 16, _____ , 18, _____ , 20

2. 11, _____ , _____ , _____ , 15, _____ , _____ , _____ , 19

3. 5, _____ , _____ , 8, _____ , _____ , 11, _____ , _____ , 14

4. _____ , _____ , 13, _____ , _____ , _____ , 17, _____ , _____ , 20

5. Connect the dots.

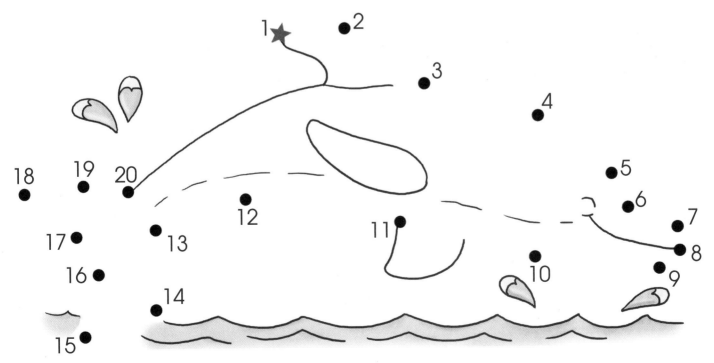

Finding Sums through 12

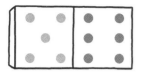

___5___ + ___6___ = ___11___

Write a number sentence about each domino.

1.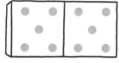

___ + ___ = ___

2.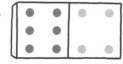

___ + ___ = ___

3.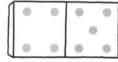

___ + ___ = ___

4.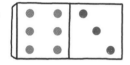

___ + ___ = ___

5.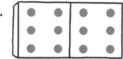

___ + ___ = ___

6.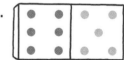

___ + ___ = ___

7.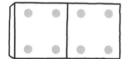

___ + ___ = ___

8.

___ + ___ = ___

9.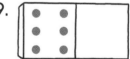

___ + ___ = ___

Draw dots on the domino to find the sum for each problem.

10.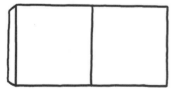

6 + 5 = ____

11.

6 + 6 = ____

12.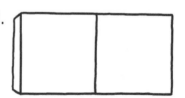

4 + 6 = ____

Addition Practice

A number line can help you find the **sum**.

$$\begin{array}{r} 7 \\ + \ 3 \\ \hline 10 \end{array}$$

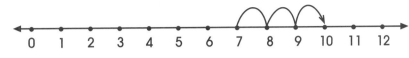

Count on **3** more than **7** to get **10**.

Find the **sums**. Use the number line if you need to.

1.
$$\begin{array}{r} 5 \\ + \ 6 \\ \hline \end{array}$$
$$\begin{array}{r} 8 \\ + \ 3 \\ \hline \end{array}$$
$$\begin{array}{r} 9 \\ + \ 1 \\ \hline \end{array}$$
$$\begin{array}{r} 4 \\ + \ 4 \\ \hline \end{array}$$

2.
$$\begin{array}{r} 7 \\ + \ 5 \\ \hline \end{array}$$
$$\begin{array}{r} 3 \\ + \ 9 \\ \hline \end{array}$$
$$\begin{array}{r} 7 \\ + \ 2 \\ \hline \end{array}$$
$$\begin{array}{r} 9 \\ + \ 2 \\ \hline \end{array}$$

3.
$$\begin{array}{r} 6 \\ + \ 6 \\ \hline \end{array}$$
$$\begin{array}{r} 7 \\ + \ 4 \\ \hline \end{array}$$
$$\begin{array}{r} 5 \\ + \ 5 \\ \hline \end{array}$$
$$\begin{array}{r} 8 \\ + \ 4 \\ \hline \end{array}$$

More Subtraction Facts

$$10 - 3 = \underline{7}$$

Look at each subtraction fact pair.
Write the **differences**.

1. $10 - 2 = \underline{\hspace{1cm}}$

    $10 - 8 = \underline{\hspace{1cm}}$

2. $12 - 8 = \underline{\hspace{1cm}}$

    $12 - 4 = \underline{\hspace{1cm}}$

3. $12 - 3 = \underline{\hspace{1cm}}$

    $12 - 9 = \underline{\hspace{1cm}}$

4. $12 - 6 = \underline{\hspace{1cm}}$

5. $12 - 5 = \underline{\hspace{1cm}}$

    $12 - 7 = \underline{\hspace{1cm}}$

6. $11 - 3 = \underline{\hspace{1cm}}$

    $11 - 8 = \underline{\hspace{1cm}}$

7. $11 - 4 = \underline{\hspace{1cm}}$

    $11 - 7 = \underline{\hspace{1cm}}$

8. $11 - 5 = \underline{\hspace{1cm}}$

    $11 - 6 = \underline{\hspace{1cm}}$

Subtraction Practice

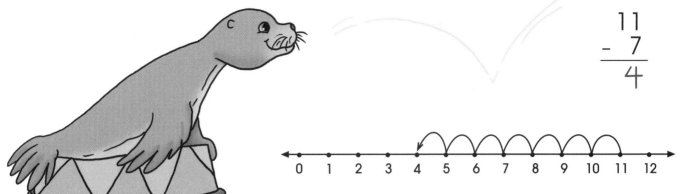

$$\begin{array}{r} 11 \\ -\ 7 \\ \hline 4 \end{array}$$

Subtract the numbers.
Write the **differences**.

1.
$$\begin{array}{r} 11 \\ -\ 5 \\ \hline \end{array}$$
$$\begin{array}{r} 10 \\ -\ 4 \\ \hline \end{array}$$
$$\begin{array}{r} 9 \\ -\ 5 \\ \hline \end{array}$$

2.
$$\begin{array}{r} 12 \\ -\ 6 \\ \hline \end{array}$$
$$\begin{array}{r} 11 \\ -\ 3 \\ \hline \end{array}$$
$$\begin{array}{r} 10 \\ -\ 2 \\ \hline \end{array}$$

3.
$$\begin{array}{r} 12 \\ -\ 4 \\ \hline \end{array}$$
$$\begin{array}{r} 11 \\ -\ 2 \\ \hline \end{array}$$
$$\begin{array}{r} 12 \\ -\ 7 \\ \hline \end{array}$$

4.
$$\begin{array}{r} 12 \\ -\ 5 \\ \hline \end{array}$$
$$\begin{array}{r} 11 \\ -\ 4 \\ \hline \end{array}$$
$$\begin{array}{r} 12 \\ -\ 8 \\ \hline \end{array}$$

Differences related to sums through 12

Do You Add or Subtract?

Write the **sum** or **difference**.

$$\begin{array}{r} 12 \\ -\ 3 \\ \hline \end{array}$$

$$\begin{array}{r} 7 \\ +\ 3 \\ \hline \end{array}$$

$$\begin{array}{r} 10 \\ -\ 4 \\ \hline \end{array}$$

$$\begin{array}{r} 9 \\ +\ 2 \\ \hline \end{array}$$

$$\begin{array}{r} 10 \\ -\ 8 \\ \hline \end{array}$$

$$\begin{array}{r} 12 \\ -\ 4 \\ \hline \end{array}$$

$$\begin{array}{r} 12 \\ -\ 7 \\ \hline \end{array}$$

$$\begin{array}{r} 8 \\ +\ 3 \\ \hline \end{array}$$

$$\begin{array}{r} 1 \\ +\ 9 \\ \hline \end{array}$$

$$\begin{array}{r} 9 \\ -\ 7 \\ \hline \end{array}$$

$$\begin{array}{r} 10 \\ -\ 3 \\ \hline \end{array}$$

$$\begin{array}{r} 7 \\ +\ 2 \\ \hline \end{array}$$

$$\begin{array}{r} 11 \\ -\ 4 \\ \hline \end{array}$$

$$\begin{array}{r} 0 \\ +\ 9 \\ \hline \end{array}$$

$$\begin{array}{r} 12 \\ -\ 6 \\ \hline \end{array}$$

$$\begin{array}{r} 5 \\ +\ 6 \\ \hline \end{array}$$

30 Addition/subtraction: sums through 12

Amazing Adding and Subtracting

Follow the path around the animals that like water.
Find the **sums** and **differences**.

3	+ 2	5	- 2	3	+ 4		+ 3	

- 1
+ 3

	+ 5		- 2		- 6	

+ 1

	- 2		- 6	

+ 4
6

Which Problems Give the Answer?

Circle the problems that give the right answer.

1. __9__   (10 - 1)   (2 + 7)   (8 + 1)   3 + 5   11 - 3

2. __5__   3 + 3   6 - 1   5 + 1   5 + 0   9 - 4

3. __8__   10 - 2   4 + 4   6 + 3   2 + 6   12 - 6

4. __10__   12 - 3   6 + 4   7 + 3   4 + 5   11 - 1

5. __12__   4 + 7   12 - 0   8 + 4   7 + 5   6 + 5

6. __6__   3 + 3   12 - 6   5 + 1   9 + 3   11 - 4

7. __11__   6 + 4   9 + 2   5 + 6   7 + 5   8 + 3

8. __7__   7 + 0   11 - 4   4 + 3   2 + 6   12 - 1

Colorful Differences

Find the **difference**.
Color the picture.

12 - 9 = _____ **Brown**

10 - 9 = _____ **Red**

11 - 9 = _____ Yellow

12 - 8 = _____ Green

12 - 6 = _____ Blue

11 - 6 = _____ **Black**

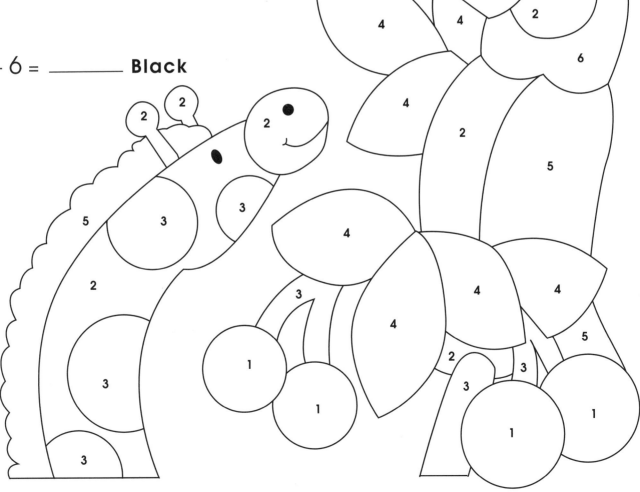

Differences related to sums through 12   **33**

Tens and Ones

tens ___1___ ones ___1___

How many? ___11___

Count the objects. Circle the objects in groups of ten.
Write the number of **tens** and **ones**. Then write how many in all.

1.

_____ tens _____ ones

How many? _____

2.

_____ tens _____ ones

How many? _____

3.

_____ tens _____ ones

How many? _____

4.

_____ tens _____ ones

How many? _____

5.

_____ tens _____ ones

How many? _____

6.

_____ tens _____ ones

How many? _____

More About Tens and Ones

_____ 2 _____ **tens**   _____ 3 _____ **ones**   tens ones
$\underline{2\ 3}$

Count the tens and ones. Write the number.

1.

_____ **tens**   _____ **ones**   tens ones
_____

2.

_____ **tens**   _____ **ones**   tens ones
_____

3.

_____ **tens**   _____ **ones**   tens ones
_____

4.

_____ **tens**   _____ **ones**   tens ones
_____

Matching Numbers with Tens and Ones

Write the number. Match the number to the correct picture.

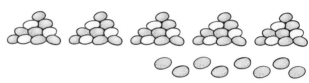

1. 2 tens 6 ones ___26___

2. 4 tens 1 one _____

3. 7 tens 0 ones _____

4. 5 tens 8 ones _____

5. 6 tens 2 ones _____

6. 8 tens 5 ones _____

7. 3 tens 7 ones _____

How Many Tens and Ones?

Read each number.
Write the number of **tens** and **ones**.

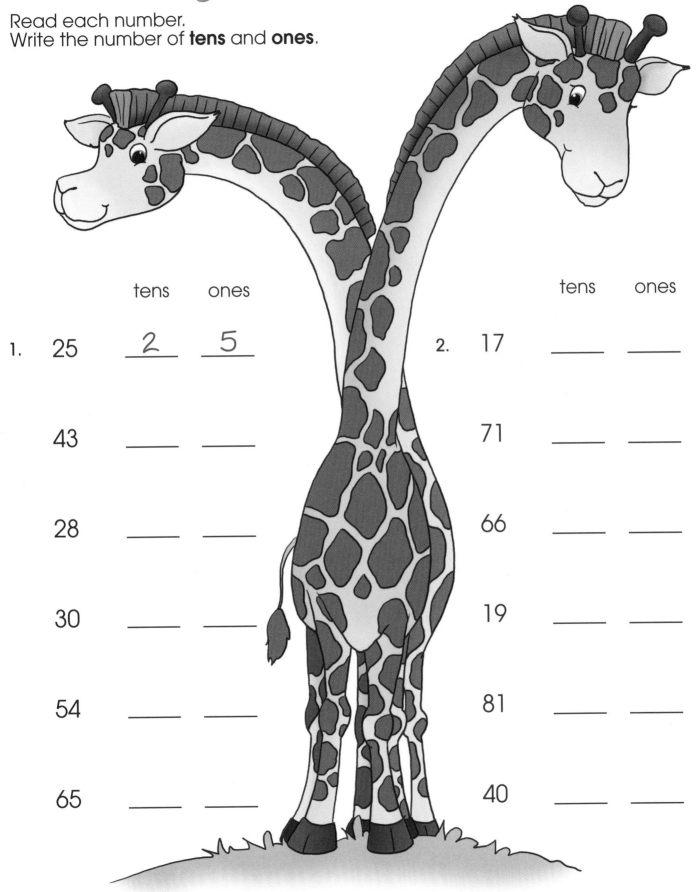

		tens	ones
1.	25	2	5
	43	___	___
	28	___	___
	30	___	___
	54	___	___
	65	___	___

		tens	ones
2.	17	___	___
	71	___	___
	66	___	___
	19	___	___
	81	___	___
	40	___	___

Place value–tens and ones

Let's Count to 100!

Count to **100**.
Write the missing numbers.

1	2								10
11	12								
				26					
		33							
				45					
							58		60
			64						
	72								
						87			
									100

Count by **2**s. Circle those squares.

Which Numbers are Missing?

Write the missing numbers in each row.

1 2 ____ 4 5 ____ 7 ____ ____ 10

41 ____ ____ ____ 45 46 ____ 48 ____ 50

____ 72 73 ____ 75 ____ ____ 78 ____ ____

31 ____ ____ ____ 35 ____ 37 ____ ____ ____

____ ____ 83 ____ ____ ____ ____ 88 ____ 90

61 ____ ____ ____ ____ ____ ____ ____ ____ 70

Counting by Ones and Tens

Start at the ▲. Connect the dots counting by **ones** to 21.
Start at the ■. Connect the dots counting by **tens** to 100.

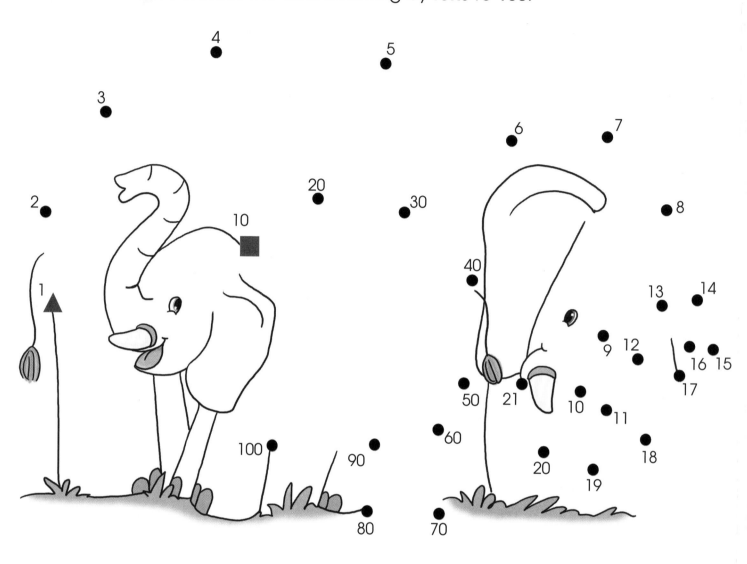

Count by **tens** to 100. Write the missing numbers.

<u> 10 </u>   _____   <u> 30 </u>   _____   _____

_____   <u> 70 </u>   _____   _____   _____

Before and After

Read each number.
Write the number that comes **before**.

1. <u> 17 </u> 18   _____ 33

2. _____ 24   _____ 67

3. _____ 81   _____ 30

4. _____ 45   _____ 27

Read each number.
Write the number that comes **after**.

5. 22 <u> 23 </u>   11 _____

6. 18 _____   37 _____

7. 27 _____   6 _____

8. 38 _____   69 _____

Comparing Tens and Ones

Write how many tens and how many ones there are.
Circle the **greater** number.

1.

<u>3</u> tens <u>2</u> ones   <u>2</u> tens <u>3</u> ones

(<u>32</u>)   <u>23</u>

2.

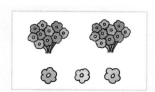 

___tens ___ones   ___tens ___ones

_____   _____

3.

___tens ___ones   ___tens ___ones

_____   _____

4.

___tens ___ones   ___tens ___ones

_____   _____

5.

 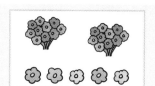

___tens ___ones   ___tens ___ones

_____   _____

6.

___tens ___ones   ___tens ___ones

_____   _____

Greater Than and Less Than

$\boxed{42}\ 24$

Circle the number that is **greater**.

1.	$\boxed{23}$	14	50	48	25	31
2.	19	21	35	27	10	15
3.	18	10	13	31	43	34

Circle the number that is **less**.

4.	55	$\boxed{48}$	25	31	23	36
5.	62	59	18	13	25	31
6.	58	69	44	54	78	82

Comparing two-digit numbers   43

Finding Sums through 15

$$\begin{array}{r} 9 \\ + 4 \\ \hline 13 \end{array}$$

0 1 2 3 4 5 6 7 8 9 10 11 12 13 14 15

Find the **sums**.

1.
$$\begin{array}{r} 8 \\ + 5 \\ \hline \end{array}$$
$$\begin{array}{r} 7 \\ + 7 \\ \hline \end{array}$$
$$\begin{array}{r} 9 \\ + 6 \\ \hline \end{array}$$
$$\begin{array}{r} 8 \\ + 4 \\ \hline \end{array}$$

2.
$$\begin{array}{r} 7 \\ + 6 \\ \hline \end{array}$$
$$\begin{array}{r} 5 \\ + 9 \\ \hline \end{array}$$
$$\begin{array}{r} 8 \\ + 7 \\ \hline \end{array}$$
$$\begin{array}{r} 6 \\ + 6 \\ \hline \end{array}$$

3.
$$\begin{array}{r} 6 \\ + 8 \\ \hline \end{array}$$
$$\begin{array}{r} 7 \\ + 5 \\ \hline \end{array}$$
$$\begin{array}{r} 4 \\ + 9 \\ \hline \end{array}$$
$$\begin{array}{r} 8 \\ + 3 \\ \hline \end{array}$$

4.
$$\begin{array}{r} 7 \\ + 4 \\ \hline \end{array}$$
$$\begin{array}{r} 9 \\ + 0 \\ \hline \end{array}$$
$$\begin{array}{r} 7 \\ + 8 \\ \hline \end{array}$$
$$\begin{array}{r} 5 \\ + 5 \\ \hline \end{array}$$

More Adding

Find the **sums**.

1. 6 + 7 = _____   4 + 9 = _____   6 + 6 = _____

2. 8 + 6 = _____   7 + 5 = _____   8 + 0 = _____

3. 7 + 8 = _____   5 + 9 = _____   7 + 7 = _____

Find the missing numbers.

4. 6 + ☐ = 14   9 + ☐ = 15   8 + ☐ = 12

5. ☐ + 7 = 13   8 + ☐ = 8   ☐ + 4 = 11

6. 3 + ☐ = 10   7 + ☐ = 15   ☐ + 9 = 14

More Subtraction Facts

Think of an addition fact to help you find the **difference**.

I know 6 + 8 =14

14 − 6 = _8_

Find the **differences**.

1. 11 − 7 = _____   13 − 9 = _____   12 − 5 = _____

2. 15 − 9 = _____   10 − 9 = _____   14 − 7 = _____

3. 12 − 3 = _____   15 − 8 = _____   13 − 8 = _____

4. 14 − 5 = _____   13 − 6 = _____   7 − 0 = _____

5. 12 − 8 = _____   9 − 9 = _____   14 − 9 = _____

6. 15 − 7 = _____   13 − 5 = _____   11 − 2 = _____

Do You Add or Subtract?

Write the **sum** or **difference**.

1.
$\begin{array}{r} 9 \\ +\ 3 \\ \hline \end{array}$
$\begin{array}{r} 11 \\ -\ 6 \\ \hline \end{array}$
$\begin{array}{r} 8 \\ +\ 7 \\ \hline \end{array}$
$\begin{array}{r} 11 \\ -\ 5 \\ \hline \end{array}$

2.
$\begin{array}{r} 12 \\ -\ 9 \\ \hline \end{array}$
$\begin{array}{r} 14 \\ -\ 6 \\ \hline \end{array}$
$\begin{array}{r} 8 \\ +\ 5 \\ \hline \end{array}$
$\begin{array}{r} 0 \\ +\ 9 \\ \hline \end{array}$

3.
$\begin{array}{r} 9 \\ +\ 6 \\ \hline \end{array}$
$\begin{array}{r} 12 \\ -\ 5 \\ \hline \end{array}$
$\begin{array}{r} 13 \\ -\ 7 \\ \hline \end{array}$
$\begin{array}{r} 12 \\ -\ 3 \\ \hline \end{array}$

4.
$\begin{array}{r} 14 \\ -\ 5 \\ \hline \end{array}$
$\begin{array}{r} 9 \\ +\ 4 \\ \hline \end{array}$
$\begin{array}{r} 8 \\ -\ 8 \\ \hline \end{array}$
$\begin{array}{r} 7 \\ +\ 7 \\ \hline \end{array}$

Finding Sums through 18

Only four more new addition facts to remember.

$8 + 8 = \underline{16}$ $8 + 9 = \underline{17}$

$9 + 7 = \underline{16}$ $9 + 9 = \underline{18}$

Find the **sums**.

1. $8 + 6 = \underline{}$ $8 + 7 = \underline{}$ $8 + 8 = \underline{}$

2. $7 + 7 = \underline{}$ $7 + 8 = \underline{}$ $7 + 9 = \underline{}$

3. $9 + 7 = \underline{}$ $9 + 8 = \underline{}$ $9 + 9 = \underline{}$

Find the **sums**.

4.
$$\begin{array}{r} 8 \\ + 5 \\ \hline \end{array} \qquad \begin{array}{r} 6 \\ + 7 \\ \hline \end{array} \qquad \begin{array}{r} 9 \\ + 6 \\ \hline \end{array} \qquad \begin{array}{r} 7 \\ + 4 \\ \hline \end{array}$$

5.
$$\begin{array}{r} 9 \\ + 8 \\ \hline \end{array} \qquad \begin{array}{r} 9 \\ + 7 \\ \hline \end{array} \qquad \begin{array}{r} 6 \\ + 8 \\ \hline \end{array} \qquad \begin{array}{r} 9 \\ + 9 \\ \hline \end{array}$$

Addition Number Wheels

Fill in each addition number wheel.
Add the outer number to the middle number.

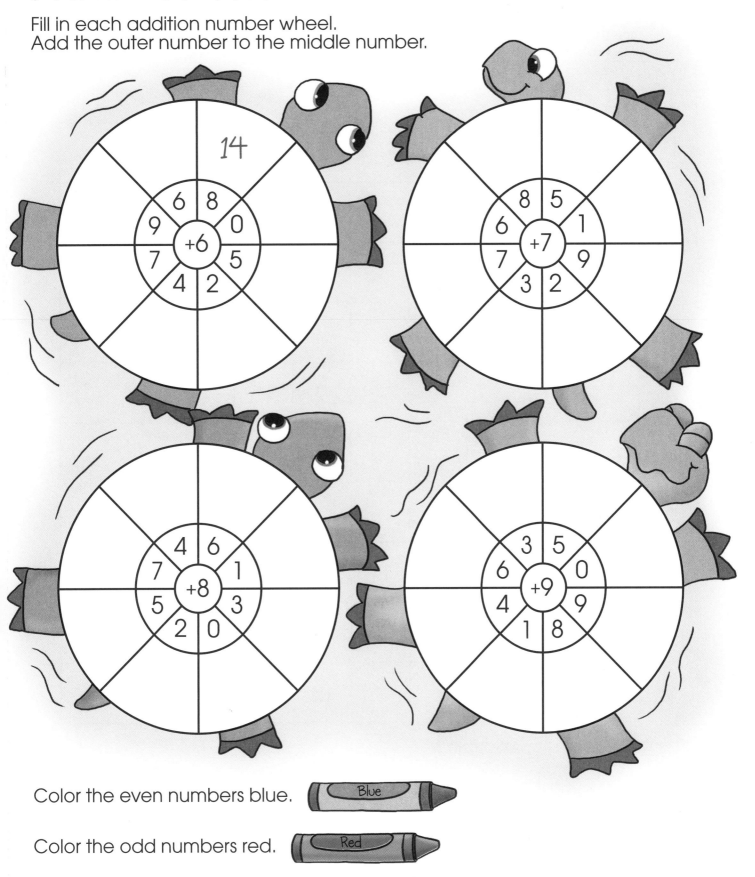

Color the even numbers blue.   Blue

Color the odd numbers red.   Red

Addition Facts Table-Sums through 18

Fill in the addition facts table by finding the **sums**.

+	0	1	2	3	4	5	6	7	8	9
0	0			3						
1								8		
2			4							
3										
4						9				
5									13	
6	6									
7				11						
8										
9			11			14				

What is the sum of each **double**?

$0 + 0 =$ _____ $1 + 1 =$ _____ $2 + 2 =$ _____ $3 + 3 =$ _____ $4 + 4 =$ _____

$5 + 5 =$ _____ $6 + 6 =$ _____ $7 + 7 =$ _____ $8 + 8 =$ _____ $9 + 9 =$ _____

Circle all the **doubles** in the addition table.

Doubles and More

If you know a **double**, it's easy to remember a **double plus 1** fact.

$7 + 7 = \underline{14}$

$7 + 8 = \underline{15}$

Find the **sums**. Use the addition facts table on page 50 if you need to.

1. $4 + 4 = \underline{}$

   $4 + 5 = \underline{}$

2. $6 + 6 = \underline{}$

   $6 + 7 = \underline{}$

3. $8 + 8 = \underline{}$

   $8 + 9 = \underline{}$

4. $5 + 5 = \underline{}$

   $5 + 6 = \underline{}$

5. $3 + 3 = \underline{}$

   $3 + 4 = \underline{}$

6. $7 + 7 = \underline{}$

   $7 + 8 = \underline{}$

Find the **sums**.

7.
$$\begin{array}{r} 6 \\ + 6 \\ \hline \end{array} \qquad \begin{array}{r} 6 \\ + 7 \\ \hline \end{array}$$

8.
$$\begin{array}{r} 7 \\ + 7 \\ \hline \end{array} \qquad \begin{array}{r} 7 \\ + 8 \\ \hline \end{array}$$

9.
$$\begin{array}{r} 5 \\ + 5 \\ \hline \end{array} \qquad \begin{array}{r} 5 \\ + 6 \\ \hline \end{array}$$

10.
$$\begin{array}{r} 8 \\ + 8 \\ \hline \end{array} \qquad \begin{array}{r} 8 \\ + 9 \\ \hline \end{array}$$

More Subtraction Facts

Look at these subtraction facts.

$16 - 9 = 7$

$16 - 7 = 9$

When you know one fact, you can think of another fact.

Write the **differences**.

1. $12 - 3 =$ _____

   $12 - 9 =$ _____

2. $14 - 5 =$ _____

   $14 - 9 =$ _____

3. $15 - 7 =$ _____

   $15 - 8 =$ _____

4. $17 - 9 =$ _____

   $17 - 8 =$ _____

5. $13 - 5 =$ _____

   $13 - 8 =$ _____

6. $11 - 6 =$ _____

   $11 - 5 =$ _____

Write the **difference**. Then write another subtraction fact using the same numbers.

7. $14 - 6 =$ _____

   $14 - 8 =$ _____

8. $17 - 8 =$ _____

   ___ - ___ = ___

9. $12 - 9 =$ _____

   ___ - ___ = ___

10. $15 - 7 =$ _____

    ___ - ___ = ___

11. $13 - 4 =$ _____

    ___ - ___ = ___

12. $15 - 9 =$ _____

    ___ - ___ = ___

Subtraction Puzzles

Fill in the squares in the diamond puzzles.

Differences related to sums through 18 53

Fact Families

$$8 + 7 = 15 \qquad 15 - 7 = 8$$
$$7 + 8 = 15 \qquad 15 - 8 = 7$$

The addition and subtraction facts are related in a **fact family**. All the facts use the same numbers.

Write the **sums**.

1. $4 + 7 =$ _____

   $7 + 4 =$ _____

   $11 - 4 =$ _____

   $11 - 7 =$ _____

2. $9 + 7 =$ _____

   $7 + 9 =$ _____

   $16 - 7 =$ _____

   $16 - 9 =$ _____

3. $7 + 0 =$ _____

   $0 + 7 =$ _____

   $7 - 0 =$ _____

   $7 - 7 =$ _____

4. $8 + 5 =$ _____

   $5 +$ _____ $= 13$

   $13 - 5 =$ _____

   $13 - 8 =$ _____

5. $8 + 9 =$ _____

   $9 + 8 =$ _____

   _____ $- 9 = 8$

   _____ $- 8 = 9$

6. $9 + 9 =$ _____

   $18 - 9 =$ _____

Write a pair of addition facts for each group of numbers.

7.   6   9   15

   ____ + ____ = ____

   ____ + ____ = ____

   ____ − ____ = ____

   ____ − ____ = ____

8.   9   9   0

   ____ + ____ = ____

   ____ + ____ = ____

   ____ − ____ = ____

   ____ − ____ = ____

9.   5   7   12

   ____ + ____ = ____

   ____ + ____ = ____

   ____ − ____ = ____

   ____ − ____ = ____

Addition and subtraction facts; sums through 18

Adding Three Numbers

Add any two numbers first. Then add the third number to find the sum.

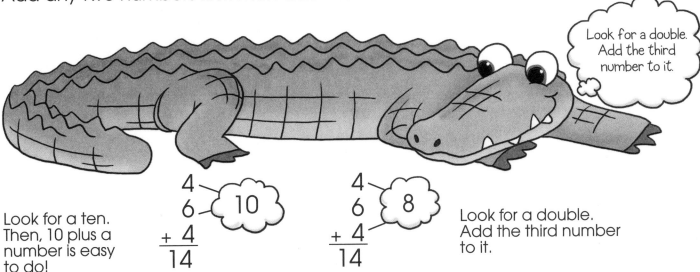

Look for a double.
Add the third
number to it.

Look for a ten.
Then, 10 plus a
number is easy
to do!

$$\begin{array}{r} 4 \\ 6 \\ +\ 4 \\ \hline 14 \end{array}$$ 10

$$\begin{array}{r} 4 \\ 6 \\ +\ 4 \\ \hline 14 \end{array}$$ 8

Look for a double.
Add the third number
to it.

Find the **sums**.

1.
$$\begin{array}{r} 3 \\ 4 \\ +\ 4 \\ \hline \end{array}$$
$$\begin{array}{r} 5 \\ 3 \\ +\ 5 \\ \hline \end{array}$$
$$\begin{array}{r} 3 \\ 7 \\ +\ 7 \\ \hline \end{array}$$
$$\begin{array}{r} 2 \\ 9 \\ +\ 2 \\ \hline \end{array}$$
$$\begin{array}{r} 4 \\ 4 \\ +\ 2 \\ \hline \end{array}$$

2.
$$\begin{array}{r} 3 \\ 9 \\ +\ 3 \\ \hline \end{array}$$
$$\begin{array}{r} 4 \\ 4 \\ +\ 4 \\ \hline \end{array}$$
$$\begin{array}{r} 3 \\ 4 \\ +\ 7 \\ \hline \end{array}$$
$$\begin{array}{r} 5 \\ 7 \\ +\ 5 \\ \hline \end{array}$$
$$\begin{array}{r} 8 \\ 0 \\ +\ 8 \\ \hline \end{array}$$

Number Riddles

Read the problem. Find the number.
Use the space to figure out the problem.

1. Start with 3.
    Double it.
    Add 8.
    What is the number? _____

2. Start with 5.
    Add 3.
    Add 9.
    What is the number? _____

3. Start with 8.
    Subtract 7.
    Add 3.
    Double it.
    What is the number? _____

4. Start with 8.
    Subtract 5.
    Add 1.
    Subtract 4
    What is the number? _____

5. Start with 4.
    Double it.
    Double it.
    What is the number? _____

Race to the Finish

This race is for 2 players.
Take turns giving the answer to every other problem. The player who has more correct answers is the winner.

GO!

3 tens + **7** ones = ____

Start

$$\begin{array}{r} 3 \\ + 9 \\ \hline \end{array}$$

$$\begin{array}{r} 6 \\ - 3 \\ \hline \end{array}$$

$$\begin{array}{r} 8 \\ + 7 \\ \hline \end{array}$$

$$\begin{array}{r} 14 \\ - 5 \\ \hline \end{array}$$

$$\begin{array}{r} 9 \\ + 8 \\ \hline \end{array}$$

$$\begin{array}{r} 12 \\ - 4 \\ \hline \end{array}$$

85 ____

$$\begin{array}{r} 8 \\ - 6 \\ \hline \end{array}$$

$$\begin{array}{r} 15 \\ - \boxed{} \\ \hline 6 \end{array}$$

$$\begin{array}{r} 8 \\ + 4 \\ \hline \end{array}$$

$$\begin{array}{r} 12 \\ - 3 \\ \hline \end{array}$$

$$\begin{array}{r} 9 \\ + 7 \\ \hline \end{array}$$

$$\begin{array}{r} 6 \\ + \boxed{} \\ \hline 15 \end{array}$$

RAH

$$\begin{array}{r} 12 \\ - 7 \\ \hline \end{array}$$

$$\begin{array}{r} 9 \\ + 5 \\ \hline \end{array}$$

$$\begin{array}{r} 8 \\ + 0 \\ \hline \end{array}$$

$$\begin{array}{r} 12 \\ - \boxed{} \\ \hline 3 \end{array}$$

$$\begin{array}{r} 10 \\ - 3 \\ \hline \end{array}$$

6 tens + 4 ones = ____

$$\begin{array}{r} 8 \\ + 8 \\ \hline \end{array}$$

$$\begin{array}{r} 15 \\ - \boxed{} \\ \hline 9 \end{array}$$

$$\begin{array}{r} 14 \\ - 5 \\ \hline \end{array}$$

$$\begin{array}{r} 13 \\ - \boxed{} \\ \hline 7 \end{array}$$

$$\begin{array}{r} 11 \\ - 7 \\ \hline \end{array}$$

$$\begin{array}{r} 9 \\ + 9 \\ \hline \end{array}$$

$$\begin{array}{r} 8 \\ + 8 \\ \hline \end{array}$$

$$\begin{array}{r} 16 \\ - \boxed{} \\ \hline 7 \end{array}$$

$$\begin{array}{r} 6 \\ + \boxed{} \\ \hline 14 \end{array}$$

$$\begin{array}{r} 9 \\ + \boxed{} \\ \hline 12 \end{array}$$

$$\begin{array}{r} 14 \\ - \boxed{} \\ \hline 5 \end{array}$$

Finish

Review numbers, addition and subtraction

What I Learned About Numbers

Write **how many** are in each group.

1.

_____

2.
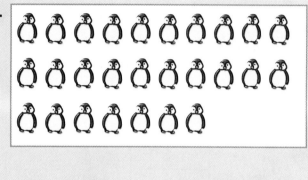

_____

Circle groups of **ten**. Count the ones. Write **how many**.

3.

_____ tens _____ ones = _____

4.
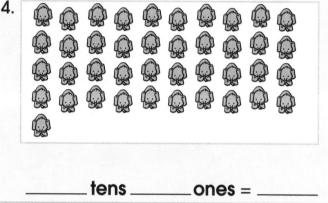

_____ tens _____ ones = _____

5. **Count** the objects in each group. Circle the group that has **less**.

_____

_____

Circle the number that is **greater**.

6.   29   37   7.   43   34   8.   69   70

Write the missing numbers.

9.   31, _____ , 33 _____ , _____ , _____ , 37, _____ , 39, _____

10.   75, _____ , _____ , 78, _____ , _____ , 81, _____ , _____ , 84

What I Learned About Facts

Find the **sums**.

1. $5 + 6 =$ _____

2. $4 + 8 =$ _____

3. $9 + 9 =$ _____

4. $7 + 0 =$ _____

5. $8 + 9 =$ _____

6. $8 + 6 =$ _____

Find the **differences**.

7. $13 - 8 =$ _____

8. $5 - 5 =$ _____

9. $14 - 7 =$ _____

10. $16 - 9 =$ _____

11. $14 - 5 =$ _____

12. $15 - 8 =$ _____

Add or **subtract**.

13.
$$\begin{array}{r} 12 \\ -5 \\ \hline \end{array}$$

14.
$$\begin{array}{r} 4 \\ +9 \\ \hline \end{array}$$

15.
$$\begin{array}{r} 8 \\ -0 \\ \hline \end{array}$$

16.
$$\begin{array}{r} 15 \\ -6 \\ \hline \end{array}$$

17.
$$\begin{array}{r} 6 \\ +6 \\ \hline \end{array}$$

18.
$$\begin{array}{r} 16 \\ -8 \\ \hline \end{array}$$

19.
$$\begin{array}{r} 3 \\ 6 \\ +7 \\ \hline \end{array}$$

20.
$$\begin{array}{r} 6 \\ 8 \\ +4 \\ \hline \end{array}$$

21. Write a **fact family** for these numbers. 7 9 16

_____ + _____ = _____   _____ – _____ = _____

_____ + _____ = _____   _____ – _____ = _____

Answer Key

Page 1

3, 5
2, 4
5, 1
7, 9

Page 2

Page 3

2 🍎🍎

6 🍌🍌🍌🍌🍌🍌

3 🍐🍐🍐

10 (pumpkins)

7 (watermelons)

5 🥕🥕🥕🥕🥕

9 (strawberries)

8 (oranges)

Page 4

0, 1, **2**, 3, **4**,
5, **6**, 7, **8**, **9**, 10,
0, **1**, **2**, 3, **4**,
5, **6**, 7, **8**, **9**, 10

Page 5

5, 7
9, 3
6, 10
8, 4

Page 6

1. 5 frogs
2. 5 birds
3. 7 fish
4. 8 bees
5. 3 giraffes
6. 10 dolphins

7. (4 fish) 4

Page 7

1. 3, ④
2. ⑥, 4
3. 5, ⑥
4. 3, ⑤
5. ⑦, 6
6. ③, 2

Page 8

1. 4 beavers
2. 2 dragon flies
3. 3 bats
4. 1 raccoon
5. 5 lightning bugs
6. 6 owls

7. (butterflies) 9

Page 9

1. 5, ③
2. ④, 6
3. ⑥, 7
4. 9, ⑦
5. 10, ⑧
6. 6, ⑤

Page 10

1. 1 + 1 = 2
2. 1 + 2 = 3
3. 1 + 3 = 4
4. 1 + 4 = 5
5. 2 + 1 = 3
6. 2 + 2 = 4
7. 2 + 3 = 5
8. 4 + 1 = 5

Page 11

1. 2   2. 1   3. 3   4. 1
   + 1   + 4   + 2   + 3
   ___   ___   ___   ___
    3   5   5   4

5. 2   6. 1   7. 2   8. 3
   + 3   + 1   + 2   + 2
   ___   ___   ___   ___
    5   2   4   5

Page 12

1. 3 − 1 = 2
2. 4 − 1 = 3
3. 4 − 2 = 2
4. 5 − 2 = 3
5. 4 − 3 = 1
6. 5 − 3 = 2
7. 3 − 2 = 1
8. 2 − 1 = 1

Page 13

1. 5   2. 5   3. 5   4. 3
   − 1   − 2   − 3   − 1
   ___   ___   ___   ___
    4   3   2   2

5. 4   6. 3   7. 2   8. 4
   − 2   − 2   − 1   − 1
   ___   ___   ___   ___
    2   1   1   3

Page 14

+	0	1	2	3	4	5
0	0	1	2	3	4	5
1	1	2	3	4	5	
2	2	3	4	5		
3	3	4	5			
4	4	5				
5	5					

Page 15

1. 4   2. 2   3. 2
4. 4   5. 5   6. 1
7. 2   8. 3   9. 5
10. 4   11. 1   12. 5   13. 3
14. 1   15. 3   16. 4   17. 3

Page 16

1. 4 + 3 = 7
2. 2 + 6 = 8
3. 2 + 7 = 9
4. 4 + 2 = 6
5. 5 + 5 = 10
6. 1 + 6 = 7
7. 6 + 4 = 10
8. 4 + 5 = 9

Page 17

1. 7   2. 7
   9   9
   8   10
  10   8

3. 8   4. 9
   9   7
   7   8
  10   10

Page 18

+	0	1	2	3	4	5	6	7	8	9
0	0	1	2	3	4	5	6	7	8	9
1	1	2	3	4	5	6	7	8	9	10
2	2	3	4	5	6	7	8	9	10	
3	3	4	5	6	7	8	9	10		
4	4	5	6	7	8	9	10			
5	5	6	7	8	9	10				
6	6	7	8	9	10					
7	7	8	9	10						
8	8	9	10							
9	9	10								

Each sum is 10

Page 19

1. 9, 9   2. 7, 7   3. 10, 10
4. 10, 10 5. 8, 8   6. 8, 8

7. 9, 5 + 4 = 9   8. 7, 4 + 3 = 7
9. 6, 0 + 6 = 6   10. 10, 2 + 8 = 10
11. 9, 9 + 0 = 9   12. 8, 7 + 1 = 8

13. 2 + 7 = 9, 7 + 2 = 9
14. 4 + 6 = 10, 6 + 4 = 10
15. 0 + 8 = 8, 8 + 0 = 8

Answer Key

Page 20

1. 5 2. 5 3. 6
4. 8 5. 6 6. 4
7. 2 8. 6 9. 0 10. 5
11. 7 12. 3 13. 2 14. 2
15. 8 – 5 = 3

Page 21

1. 4, 3 2. 4, 5 3. 7, 0
4. 8, 1 5. 8, 2 6. 2, 6
7. 4, 9 – 4 = 5 8. 2, 7 – 2 = 5
9. 6, 6 – 6 = 0 10. 8, 10 – 8 = 2
11. 0, 8 – 0 = 8 12. 7, 8 – 7 = 1
13. 9 – 3 = 6, 9 – 6 = 3
14. 10 – 2 = 8, 10 – 8 = 2
15. 9 – 0 = 9, 9 – 9 = 0

Page 22

Page 23

1. 9 2. 5 3. 9
4. 9 5. 9 6. 5
7. 8 8. 9 9. 10
10. 10 11. 4 12. 7 13. 7
14. 3 15. 10 16. 10 17. 6

Page 24

1. 10 and 5, 15
2. 10 and 7, 17
3. 10 and 10, 20
4. 10 and 3, 13
5. 10 and 6, 16
6. 10 and 1, 11

Page 25

1. 11, 12, **13**, 14, **15**, 16, **17**, 18, **19**, 20
2. 11, **12**, **13**, **14**, 15, **16**, **17**, **18**, 19
3. 5, **6**, **7**, 8, **9**, **10**, 11, **12**, **13**, 14
4. 11, **12**, 13, **14**, **15**, **16**, 17, **18**, **19**, 20

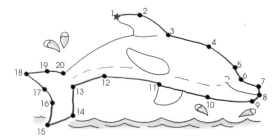

Page 26

1. 5 + 5 = 10 2. 6 + 4 = 10 3. 4 + 5 = 9
4. 6 + 3 = 9 5. 6 + 6 = 12 6. 6 + 5 = 11
7. 4 + 4 = 8 8. 2 + 6 = 8 9. 6 + 0 = 6
10. 6 + 5 = 11 11. 6 + 6 = 12
12. 4 + 6 = 10

Page 27

1. 11, 11, 10, 8
2. 12, 12, 9, 11
3. 12, 11, 10, 12

Page 28

1. 8, 2 2. 4, 8
3. 9, 3 4. 6
5. 7, 5 6. 8, 3
7. 7, 4 8. 6, 5

Page 29

1. 6, 6, 4,
2. 6, 8, 8,
3. 8, 9, 5,
4. 7, 7, 4,

Page 30

Page 31

Answer Key

Page 32
1. Answer given
2. 6 - 1, 5 + 0, 9 - 4
3. 10 - 2, 4 + 4, 2 + 6
4. 6 + 4, 7 + 3, 11 - 1
5. 12 - 0, 8 + 4, 7 + 5
6. 3 + 3, 12 - 6, 5 + 1
7. 9 + 2, 5 + 6, 8 + 3
8. 7 + 0, 11 - 4, 4 + 3

Page 33
3 Brown
1 Red
2 Yellow
4 Green
6 Blue
5 Black

Page 34
1. 2, 5, 25
2. 2, 6, 26
3. 3, 8, 38
4. 3, 4, 34
5. 2, 8, 28
6. 3, 0, 30

Page 35
1. 5, 6, 56
2. 3, 2, 32
3. 4, 7, 47
4. 6, 8, 68

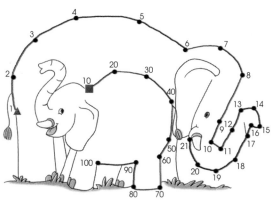

Page 36
1. 2 tens 6 ones __26__
2. 4 tens 1 one __41__
3. 7 tens 0 ones __70__
4. 5 tens 8 ones __58__
5. 6 tens 2 ones __62__
6. 8 tens 5 ones __85__
7. 3 tens 7 ones __37__

Page 37
1. | tens | ones |
   |------|------|
   | 2 | 5 |
   | 4 | 3 |
   | 2 | 8 |
   | 3 | 0 |
   | 5 | 4 |
   | 6 | 5 |

2. | tens | ones |
   |------|------|
   | 1 | 7 |
   | 7 | 1 |
   | 6 | 6 |
   | 1 | 9 |
   | 8 | 1 |
   | 4 | 0 |

Page 38

1	②	3	④	5	⑥	7	⑧	9	⑩
11	⑫	13	⑭	15	⑯	17	⑱	19	⑳
21	㉒	23	㉔	25	㉖	27	㉘	29	㉚
31	㉜	33	㉞	35	㊱	37	㊳	39	㊵
41	㊷	43	㊹	45	㊻	47	㊽	49	㊿
51	52	53	54	55	56	57	58	59	60
61	62	63	64	65	66	67	68	69	70
71	72	73	74	75	76	77	78	79	80
81	82	83	84	85	86	87	88	89	90
91	92	93	94	95	96	97	98	99	100

Page 39

1	2	**3**	4	5	**6**	7	**8**	**9**	10
41	**42**	**43**	**44**	45	46	**47**	48	**49**	50
71	72	73	**74**	75	**76**	**77**	78	**79**	**80**
31	**32**	33	34	35	**36**	37	**38**	**39**	**40**
81	82	83	**84**	**85**	86	87	**88**	**89**	90
61	**62**	**63**	**64**	**65**	**66**	**67**	**68**	**69**	70

Page 40

10	**20**	30	**40**	**50**
60	70	**80**	**90**	**100**

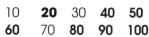

Page 41

Before
1. 17, 32
2. 23, 66
3. 80, 29
4. 44, 26
After
5. 23, 12
6. 19, 38
7. 28, 7
8. 39, 70

Page 42
1. 3 tens 2 ones   2 tens 3 ones   2. 2 tens 4 ones   2 tens 7 ones
   (32)   23   24   (27)
3. 3 tens 5 ones   2 tens 9 ones   4. 4 tens 3 ones   3 tens 4 ones
   (35)   29   (43)   34
5. 1 tens 5 ones   2 tens 5 ones   6. 5 tens 0 ones   4 tens 1 ones
   15   (25)   (50)   41

Page 43
Greater
1. 23, 50, 31
2. 21, 35, 15
3. 18, 31, 43
Less
4. 48, 25, 23
5. 59, 13, 25
6. 58, 44, 78

Page 44
1. 13, 14, 15, 12
2. 13, 14, 15, 12
3. 14, 12, 13, 11
4. 11, 9, 15, 10

Page 45
1. 13, 13, 12
2. 14, 12, 8
3. 15, 14, 14
4. 8, 6, 4
5. 6, 0, 7
6. 7, 8, 5

Page 46
1. 4, 4, 7
2. 6, 1, 7
3. 9, 7, 5
4. 9, 7, 7
5. 4, 0, 5
6. 8, 8, 9

Page 47
1. 12, 5, 15, 6
2. 3, 8, 13, 9
3. 15, 7, 6, 9
4. 9, 13, 0, 14

Page 48
1. 14, 15, 16
2. 14, 15, 16
3. 16, 17, 18
4. 13, 13, 15, 11
5. 17, 16, 14, 18

Answer Key

Page 49

Page 50

+	0	1	2	3	4	5	6	7	8	9
0	⓪	1	2	3	4	5	6	7	8	9
1	1	②	3	4	5	6	7	8	9	10
2	2	3	④	5	6	7	8	9	10	11
3	3	4	5	⑥	7	8	9	10	11	12
4	4	5	6	7	⑧	9	10	11	12	13
5	5	6	7	8	9	⑩	11	12	13	14
6	6	7	8	9	10	11	⑫	13	14	15
7	7	8	9	10	11	12	13	⑭	15	16
8	8	9	10	11	12	13	14	15	⑯	17
9	9	10	11	12	13	14	15	16	17	⑱

$0+0=\underline{0}$ $1+1=\underline{2}$ $2+2=\underline{4}$ $3+3=\underline{6}$ $4+4=\underline{8}$

$5+5=\underline{10}$ $6+6=\underline{12}$ $7+7=\underline{14}$ $8+8=\underline{16}$ $9+9=\underline{18}$

Page 51

1. 8, 9 **2.** 12,13 **3.** 16,17
4. 10, 11 **5.** 6, 7 **6.** 14,15
7. 12, 13 **8.** 14,15
9. 10, 11 **10.** 16,17

Page 52

1. 9,3 **2.** 9,5 **3.** 8,7
4. 8,9 **5.** 8,5 **6.** 5,6
7. 8, $14 - 8 = 6$
8. 9, $17 - 9 = 8$
9. 3, $12 - 3 = 9$
10. 8, $15 - 8 = 7$
11. 9, $13 - 9 = 4$
12. 6, $15 - 6 = 9$

Page 53

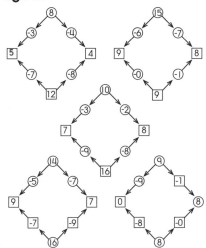

Page 54

1. 11, 11, 7, 4
2. 16, 16, 9, 7
3. 7, 7, 7, 0
4. 13, 8, 8, 5
5. 17, 17, 17, 17
6. 18, 9
7. $6 + 9 = 15$ **8.** $9 + 0 = 9$ **9.** $5 + 7 = 12$
   $9 + 6 = 15$ $0 + 9 = 9$ $7 + 5 = 12$
   $15 - 6 = 9$ $9 - 0 = 9$ $12 - 5 = 7$
   $15 - 9 = 6$ $9 - 9 = 9$ $12 - 7 = 5$

Page 55

1. 11, 13, 17, 13, 10
2. 15, 12, 14, 17, 16

Page 56

1. 14
2. 17
3. 8
4. 0
5. 16

Page 57

Page 58

1. 9   **2.** 16
3. 2, 7, 27 **4.** 4, 1, 41
5. ㉓,33 **6.** 29 ㊲
7. ㊸ 34 **8.** 69 ㊹
9. 31, **32**, 33, **34, 35, 36**, 37, **38**, 39, **40**
10. 75, **76, 77**, 78, **79, 80**, 81, **82, 83**, 84

Page 59

1. 11 **2.** 12 **3.** 18
4. 7 **5.** 17 **6.** 14
7. 5 **8.** 0 **9.** 7
10. 7 **11.** 9 **12.** 7
13. 7 **14.** 13 **15.** 8 **16.** 9
17. 12 **18.** 8 **19.** 16 **20.** 18
21. $7 + 9 = 16$
   $9 + 7 = 16$
   $16 - 7 = 9$
   $16 - 9 = 7$

Math Award

Great Job!

_____
Name

finished Math 1

from

School Zone Publishing.